Blue Ribbon Day

D0188811

I Can Read Book® is a trademark of HarperCollins Publishers.

Pony Scouts: Blue Ribbon Day. Copyright © 2013 by HarperCollins Publishers. All rights reserved. Manufactured in China. No part of this book may be used or reproduced in any manner without written permission except in the case of brief quotations embodied in critical articles and reviews. For information address HarperCollins Children's Books, a division of HarperCollins Publishers, 10 East 53rd Street, New York, NY 10022. www.icanread.com

Library of Congress catalog card number: 2012949621
ISBN 978-0-06-208677-8 (trade bdg.)—ISBN 978-0-06-208676-1 (pbk.)
Typography by Sean Boggs

13 14 15 16 17   SCP   10 9 8 7 6 5 4 3 2 1   ❖   First Edition

I Can Read!

READING 2 WITH HELP

PONY SCOUTS

Blue Ribbon Day

by Catherine Hapka
pictures by Anne Kennedy

HARPER
An Imprint of HarperCollinsPublishers

Jill, Meg, and Annie
were best friends.
They loved horses and ponies so much
that they called themselves
the Pony Scouts.
Today they were going
to the county fair.

anythink
NO LONGER PROPERTY

Dear Parent:
Your child's love of reading starts here!

Every child learns to read in a different way and at his or her own speed. Some go back and forth between reading levels and read favorite books again and again. Others read through each level in order. You can help your young reader improve and become more confident by encouraging his or her own interests and abilities. From books your child reads with you to the first books he or she reads alone, there are I Can Read Books for every stage of reading:

SHARED READING
Basic language, word repetition, and whimsical illustrations, ideal for sharing with your emergent reader

BEGINNING READING
Short sentences, familiar words, and simple concepts for children eager to read on their own

READING WITH HELP
Engaging stories, longer sentences, and language play for developing readers

READING ALONE
Complex plots, challenging vocabulary, and high-interest topics for the independent reader

ADVANCED READING
Short paragraphs, chapters, and exciting themes for the perfect bridge to chapter books

I Can Read Books have introduced children to the joy of reading since 1957. Featuring award-winning authors and illustrators and a fabulous cast of beloved characters, I Can Read Books set the standard for beginning readers.

A lifetime of discovery begins with the magical words **"I Can Read!"**

Visit www.icanread.com for information
on enriching your child's reading experience.

"Are we there yet?" Meg asked.

Jill's mom smiled at the girls.

"We'll be there soon," she said.

Jill's mom owned a pony farm.

She was entering two ponies

in a driving class at the fair.

When they got to the fair

Meg didn't know where to look first.

She saw animals everywhere.

She smelled lots of tasty food.

She heard different kinds of music.

The horse barn was busy.

"That's the smallest pony

I've ever seen!" Meg cried.

"Her name is Bubbles,"

a woman said with a smile.

"She's a miniature horse."

"She's so cute!" Jill said.

"That horse is huge!" Annie said.

"It's a shire," Jill's mom told her.

"That's a breed of draft horse."

A boy was standing nearby.

"His name is Champ," he said.

"He's going to win the driving class."

"No way!" Meg said.

"Jill's mom is going to win!"

"Don't count on it," the boy said.

"Champ always wins."

"Come here please, Ben!"

a woman called.

"I have to go," the boy said.

"But I'll see you later,

when Champ wins the blue ribbon."

"Enjoy the fair, but please be back by two o'clock," Jill's mom told the girls.

"Let's see more animals," Jill said.

"Let's eat," Meg suggested.

Annie smiled. "Let's do both!"

There were animals everywhere!

The girls watched a cow get a bath.

They saw a sheep being sheared.

They cheered for a prize pig

and laughed at a fancy rooster.

There was food everywhere, too.

Jill ate a corn dog.

Annie tasted a funnel cake.

Meg ate one of each,

plus some cotton candy.

Then the girls rode a Ferris wheel.

"Whee!" Jill cried. "This is fun!"

"I've never been up so high before!"
Annie exclaimed.

"I'm still hungry," Meg said.

"Let's try some curly fries next."

"Okay," Jill said.

"But we need to go back soon."

The girls were petting a baby goat
when they saw Ben coming.
"Hi," he said.
"Did you come to watch me
win the pie-eating contest?"

Meg was tired of Ben's bragging.

"A pie-eating contest?" she said.

"That sounds like fun.

Get ready for us to beat you!"

Soon the contest started.

Annie was full from the curly fries.

She barely finished one piece of pie.

Jill dropped out after two pieces.

"I'm stuffed!" She moaned.

"This pie is delicious!" Meg said.

She finished her third piece

and then her fourth.

"Meg and Ben are in the finals!"

the announcer said.

"Go, Meg, go!" Meg's friends chanted.

But Meg was feeling very full.

The pie didn't taste as good now.

She couldn't eat another bite.

"I give up," she said.

"I win!" Ben yelled.

"And pretty soon

Champ will win, too!"

Jill checked the time.

"We have to go!" she said.

"Hurry!" Meg cried.

"We have to get back to help
get the ponies ready!"
The girls rushed away from
the pie-eating contest.

They hurried past the Ferris wheel
and the curly fry stand.
They dashed through the barn
full of chickens and pigs
and sheep and cows.

Finally the girls burst into

the horse barn.

"We're here!" Meg cried.

"Hello, girls," Jill's mom said.

"You're right on time."

The girls went to work.

They groomed Inky and Smoky.

Then they helped Jill's mom

put on the harness

and hook the ponies to a cart.

The Pony Scouts cheered as Jill's mom

drove Inky and Smoky around the ring.

They cheered even more when

Inky and Smoky won the blue ribbon!

"Hooray!" Meg cheered.

She wanted to tease Ben

the way he had teased her.

But she knew it wouldn't be nice.

"Champ was great," she said instead.

"He won second place!"

Ben looked surprised.

His mother smiled at Meg.

"Thank you, dear," she said.

"You're a good sport."

"Yeah," Ben muttered. "Thanks."

Later, the girls got ready to leave.

"I love the county fair!" Jill said.

"Me, too," Annie agreed.

Meg just nodded and burped.

The Pony Scouts couldn't wait

to come to the fair again next year!

PONY POINTERS

driving class: a show class where horses or ponies pull a cart or carriage instead of being ridden

draft horse: a large type of horse often bred to pull a cart or plow

shire: one breed of draft horse (other draft breeds include Belgian, Percheron, and Clydesdale)

harness: the straps that connect a horse or pony to a cart or carriage